On the Rop

The ultimate wrestling quiz

CONTENTS

INTRODUCTION

Welcome to On the Ropes, a quizbook that covers a diverse range of topics across the wonderful world of professional wrestling. The book is aimed at both casual fans and more hardcore enthusiasts, with questions covering a huge range of promotions, eras and styles. Some quizzes will be straightforward, others offer more of a challenge and require a little more specialist knowledge!

In addition to more than 600 general knowledge questions, we've included a series of challenges and puzzles – match the wrestler to their hometown, identify grapplers from their real names, list the first 10 holders of a particular belt or achievement, identify tag teams from their members, and more. We'll cover American, British, Japanese, Canadian and Mexican wrestling, take in the greatest stars of yesteryear and test your knowledge of the big names plying their trade in the ring right now.

Whatever your level of wrestling knowledge, On the Ropes is designed to entertain and educate – have fun!

Paul and Toby

THE OPENING BELL

Learning the basics

Here is a quick selection of general wrestling questions to get you started. No special moves, no double-teams, no high-flying trick questions at this stage!

1. What do the initials WWE stand for?

2. Steve Austin became a global star during the "Attitude Era". By what nickname is this wrestler usually known?

3. Which family owns the largest stake in the WWE?

4. What is the name of the WWE's biggest annual show, held each Spring?

5. Hulk Hogan famously told us to say our prayers and take our ... what?

6. From which country does WWE star Rusev hail?

7. In classic 1980's British wrestling, who was Big Daddy's bitter rival?

8. What is the name of the most popular current promotion in Japan?

9. What is the name of an event in which multiple wrestlers appear, and the only way to be eliminated is to be thrown over the top rope?

10. Which animal completes this famous tag team: the British _____?

GENERAL TRIVIA 1

A little bit of everything

Before we move onto more specialized questions, let's check out your general wrestling knowledge a little more!

1. Which animal did Jake Roberts usually bring to the ring? For a bonus, what was the name of his most iconic pet?

2. Which cable network aired WWE's "Brawl to End it All" in 1984 and "The War to Settle the Score" in 1985?

3. How many competitors took part in 2018's Greatest Royal Rumble?

4. Which wrestler won an Olympic gold medal with a "broken freaking neck"?

5. Which former wrestling superstar has appeared in hit films such as Central Intelligence and Jumanji?

6. In which year was the first episode of Smackdown?

7. Which legendary Japanese wrestler competed in a match with Muhammad Ali?

8. Who was the winner of the first Mae Young Classic women's tournament?

9. Which outspoken manager famously formed a commentary team with Gorilla Monsoon?

10. Which multiple-time world and tag team champion was forced to retire in April 2011 due to a neck injury?

"FROM PARTS UNKNOWN"

Where do they come from?

A wrestler's ring introduction usually includes their name, weight and where they come from. Can you name the wrestling star whose introduction usually included the following remarks?

1. Which all-time great hailed from "Grenoble, in the French Alps ..."

2. Which legendary 1980s star was often introduced with the line "From Venice Beach, California, weighing 302 pounds"

3. Which current WWE star is announced as "From Bulgaria, weighing 138 kilos"

4. Which Mick Foley alter ego came from Truth or Consequences, New Mexico?

5. Which mysterious wrestler was said to come from "Death Valley, California, weighing 310 pounds"?

6. Which WWE women's star hails from "the Queen city"?

7. Which Ed Leslie persona was billed as "From the Land of Yin and Yang"?

8. Which tag team came from Cameron, North Carolina?

9. Name the current female WWE star that hails from Columbus, Ohio?

10. Which WCW star was bizarrely said to hail "From the Outer Reaches of Your Mind!"

WRESTLEMANIA HIGHLIGHTS

Recalling events at the WWE's biggest show

The Showcase of the Immortals, the grandest stage of them all! WrestleMania has seen its fair share of classic matches and iconic moments, now test your knowledge of the WWE's flagship annual event!

1. Which legendary boxer was a special guest referee at the first WrestleMania?

2. The performance of which song typically opens each show?

3. Who ended the Undertaker's twenty-year winning streak?

4. Which three teams competed in the incredible TLC match at WrestleMania X-7?

5. Which icon defeated Hulk Hogan at Toronto's WrestleMania 6 in 1990?

6. At which WrestleMania did Vince McMahon have his head shaved by Donald Trump?

7. Which tag team hosted WrestleMania 33 in Orlando?

8. At WrestleMania 30, which three all-time legends shared a beer in the ring?

9. Which two stars engaged in a 60-minute Iron man match at WrestleMania 12?

10. Which controversial sporting superstar famously refereed the match between Stone Cold Steve Austin and Shawn Michaels in 1998?

BIG IN JAPAN

How well do you know the stars of the Orient?

Japan has long been a home of high-impact, high-quality wrestling. From the legendary Inoki and Baba to modern stars like Nakamura, Omega and Okada. Let's see how well you know your Japanese grappling!

1. What does AJPW stand for?

2. Japanese star Shohei Baba was best known by which nickname?

3. Which of the following American stars has not won the IWGP heavyweight title – Hulk Hogan, Brock Lesnar, Steve Austin, AJ Styles?

4. Under what name did current WWE star Finn Balor mainly wrestle in Japan?

5. Which masked Japanese high-flying superstar won the Super J Cup in 1995 and memorably feuded with Brian Pillman in WCW?

6. Which All Japan great tragically died in the ring in 2009?

7. Which New Japan faction, typically composed of gaijin (foreign wrestlers), has been led by AJ Styles, Cody Rhodes and Kenny Omega?

8. Keiji Mutoh wrestled both under his own name and as which alter-ego?

9. Kota Ibushi and Kenny Omega formed a tag team known by what romantic name?

10. Which American brothers won two IWGP tag team titles in the early 1990s?

WHO ARE YOU?

Match the real name to their wrestling persona

Most wrestlers adopt a new persona when they enter the wrestling world; this often changes multiple times through their careers. Do you know the wrestling names by which these real-life figures are best known?

1. Mark Calaway

2. Jim Hellwig

3. Richard Blood

4. Glen Jacobs

5. Ashley Fliehr

6. Joe Anoa'i

7. Pamela Rose Martinez

8. Jay Reso

9. Virgil Runnels Jr

10. Leon White

BRITISH INVASION

Celebrating British successes in the US and Japan

Britain has a long and proud tradition of wrestling greatness. Many of its finest stars also made their way to compete in North America and Japan. Here are 10 questions to test your knowledge of these stars!

1. The Dynamite Kid, a huge star in Japan, Canada and the US, hails from which Lancashire town?

2. Giant Haystacks briefly appeared in the WWF using what nickname?

3. Female star Saraya-Jade Bevis is better known by what name in the WWE?

4. Which retired British wrestler is the on-air general manager of NXT?

5. Steve Austin was trained by, and later feuded with, which English wrestler?

6. Which well-spoken Englishman regularly co-presented WWF TV events in the 1980s alongside Gorilla Monsoon and Vince McMahon?

7. Which Welshman has released numerous autobiographies and wrestled using the nickname "Exotic"?

8. Which young high-flying British star captured the IWGP junior heavyweight championship in 2017 and again in 2018?

9. Which moustachioed Manchester grappler joined the WWE main roster in 2017 and was noted for carrying an umbrella to the ring?

10. Who was the first WWE UK champion?

THE WOMEN'S REVOLUTION

Making history ... again

Much has been said about the women's "revolution" in the WWE during recent years. How much do you know about the wrestlers and events involved?

1. Which British wrestler was the first to hold the NXT women's title?

2. From which country do Emma, Peyton Royce and Billie Kay hail?

3. Which Japanese star remained undefeated as NXT women's champion until giving up the belt in 2017?

4. Who is Sasha Banks' famous musical cousin?

5. Becky Lynch was once trained by which current WWE main roster star?

6. Alexa Bliss was the first woman to hold the NXT, Raw and SmackDown women's titles – true or false?

7. Who did Bayley defeat to become NXT women's champion, and who did she defeat to win the Raw women's title?

8. Liv Morgan and Sarah Logan form two thirds of which current Raw faction?

9. What is Japanese star Asuka's regal-sounding nickname?

10. Which female wrestler trains many of the women at the NXT Performance Center?

NXT! NXT!

The development brand with star quality all its own

Originally envisaged as a developmental brand, NXT has taken on a life of its own, thanks to standout events and some of the best matches in all of pro wrestling. See if you can answer ten questions about this upstart promotion!

1. NXT moved to the Full Sail University Performance Center in which year?

2. What is the recurring name of the NXT's quarterly pay-per-view event?

3. Seth Rollins was the first NXT champion – who did he beat in a tournament final to capture the belt?

4. Which member of the Four Horsewomen did not capture the NXT Women's championship?

5. Before their incredible 2017/18 feud, Johnny Gargano and Tommaso Ciampa formed which popular tag team?

6. Which city borough has hosted four successive August TakeOver events?

7. The NXT tag team tournament is named after which wrestling legend?

8. Who became the first NXT North American Champion in April 2018?

9. Which team held the NXT tag belts for the longest time?

10. Which faction included Eric Young, Nikki Cross and Killian Dane?

GENERAL TRIVIA 2

A little bit of everything

Time to get back to basics and discover how many questions about general wrestling trivia you can answer!

1. The RKO is a finisher for Randy Orton, but what does it stand for?

2. How many world titles has Shawn Michaels won?

3. Which colourful wrestler's gimmick was based on Elvis Presley?

4. Which WWE legend mocked Roman Reigns for forgetting his lines during a 2017 RAW promo?

5. Enzo Amore and Big Cass debuted as a tag team on the main WWE roster in which year?

6. Which future US president featured on Raw and WrestleMania, famously shaving Vince McMahon's hair off?

7. Who was the first wrestler to be inducted into the WWF Hall of Fame?

8. One of Chris Jericho's recent gimmicks was his light-up jacket. Who destroyed it?

9. In which year did Hulk Hogan win his 2nd WWF heavyweight title?

10. Who was the first undisputed WWE champion?

BITTER ENEMIES

Love and hate in the ring

Wrestling is defined by its iconic rivalries. While the good guy / bad guy roles have been very much blurred over the past few years, strong rivalries underpin many of the wrestling world's biggest stories.

1. In the 1990s WWF and WCW engaged in a long-running feud known as what?

2. How many times did The Rock and Steve Austin face off at WrestleMania?

3. Which brothers famously competed against each other in the opening match at WrestleMania 10?

4. Which monstrous WCW champion enjoyed a violent rivalry with Cactus Jack in the early 1990s?

5. Kevin Steen and El Generico set the independent scene alight. By what names are these two on/off rivals better known in WWE?

6. The Hart Foundation had a huge rivalry with which UK team?

7. Who finally defeated Kazuchika Okada in 2018 to capture the IWGP title after a series of incredible encounters?

8. Which outspoken Iranian wrestler and former WWF champion has engaged in online rivalries with numerous current and former stars?

9. Britain's Dynamite Kid had an amazing rivalry in New Japan in the 1980s against which comic book inspired character?

10. Al Snow and the Big Bossman once feuded over Al's dog. What was it called?

THE MONDAY NIGHT WARS

WCW v WWF

Bischoff vs McMahon. WWF vs WCW. Monday Nitro vs Monday Night RAW. The heated Monday Night Wars sparked furious debate among fans, wrestlers and commentators. How much can you recall about the amazing rivalry?

1. Before joining forces with Hulk Hogan, how were the rebellious team of Scott Hall and Kevin Nash better known when they first arrived in WCW?

2. How did Madusa Miceli shock the world when she showed up on Nitro?

3. The nWo typically did what to the bodies of defeated opponents?

4. Starting in 1994, Monday Nitro broadcast from which Orlando studio?

5. Which controversial writer, best known for his shock storylines, worked for both organisations during the Wars?

6. Which dominant character did WCW introduce as a direct rival to the WWF's Steve Austin?

7. Which WWF world title change was famously "spoiled" on Nitro, leading to many viewers switching channels to watch?

8. Which two wrestlers were involved in the infamous 'Fingerpoke of Doom'?

9. For how many consecutive weeks did Nitro defeat Raw in the TV ratings?

10. Which former WCW world champion and bodybuilder shockingly appeared on the first Nitro broadcast, having returned from the WWF days before?

YOU DESERVE IT ...

Getting the crowd involved

The live audience at a wrestling event can often make or break that show. Which superstars have received the following chants from the audience?

1. Which NXT and WWE women's champion is often serenaded to a version of "Hey Baby"?

2. Which WWE personality is greeted by the crowd chanting "You Suck" in time to his music?

3. The Dudley Boyz would often hear which chant during their matches, in anticipation of their wild antics?

4. Fans often chant "What?" at the end of every sentence to put off a wrestler during a promo. But which iconic star began the craze in the Attitude Era?

5. Which father and daughter receive trademark "wooo!" calls during their entrances and matches?

6. Which female star also uses Daniel Bryan's "Yes! Yes! Yes!" chant?

7. Seth Rollins referred to which charismatic star as "Sparkle Crotch", leading to a huge crowd reaction?

8. Which feuding NXT stars regularly received chants of "Fight Forever" during their brutal 2017 and 2018 encounters?

9. Which hard-hitting promotion's fans would regularly chant its name during more extreme moments of action?

10. Which Spanish word is often chanted at Sami Zayn during his entrance?

HOGAN AND FLAIR

1980s legends raise the bar

Bruno Sammartino was undoubtedly the predominant wrestling star of the 1960s and 1970s, with a no-nonsense style and huge popular appeal. In the following decade, two new stars emerged – enter Hulk Hogan and Ric Flair.

1. From which controversial wrestler did Hulk Hogan capture his first WWF title in 1984?

2. Complete the Ric Flair quote: "To be the man ..."

3. In 1988 Hogan formed the Megapowers with which charismatic superstar?

4. In 1981, Flair captured his first NWA world title against which colourful character?

5. Flair traded the NWA world title with which member of the Von Erich family?

6. To whom did Hogan controversially lose his world championship during 1988's Main Event TV broadcast?

7. Against which movie character turned wrestler did Hogan feud during the summer of 1989?

8. Which future world champion wrestled Flair to a 45-minute draw at the first Clash of the Champions in 1988?

9. Hogan fought in four singles matches at WrestleMania during the 1980s – who were his opponents?

10. Which three stars did Flair face at the 1989 Starrcade Iron Man tournament?

THE HEARTBREAK KID

He's just a boy toy ...

Shawn Michaels is universally recognized as one of the greatest in-ring competitors in pro wrestling history. How much can you recall about Shawn's career?

1. At WrestleMania 10 Michaels competed in a famous ladder match against which close friend?

2. Who was his tag team partner in the Rockers?

3. Who did Michaels beat to capture his first WWF world heavyweight title?

4. Which legend did Michaels "retire" at WrestleMania 24?

5. In early 1997, Michaels forfeited his WWF title, claiming an injury and that he had lost what?

6. When Michaels turned against his former partner in the Rockers, he threw him through a glass window during which WWF talk show?

7. At which two WrestleMania events did Michaels face the Undertaker in classic matches?

8. What is his real name?

9. Which future world champion acted as Michaels' bodyguard in the mid-1990s?

10. In which year and by whom was Michaels inducted into the WWE Hall of Fame?

TABLES, LADDERS AND CHAIRS (OH MY)

Celebrating the best of TLC

Wrestling's most exciting matches often involve one or all of tables, ladders and chairs. Let's see what you can recall of these memorable events!

1. Razor Ramon and Shawn Michaels competed in a ladder match at which WrestleMania event?

2. Which three teams competed in famed TLC events during the Attitude Era?

3. Which annual pay per view event has men's and women's ladder matches?

4. At Summerslam 2001, which two high flying stars competed in a ladder match for the Hardcore Championship?

5. In 1972, which wrestling organisation held the first official ladder match?

6. In June 2008, who did Edge defeat in a TLC match to win the WWE title?

7. Which two competitors fought for the Smackdown women's title in a ladder match at TLC 2016?

8. In December 1999 which two stars traded the WCW US Heavyweight title in a pair of ladder matches?

9. Which charismatic duo won the Ring of Honor tag team titles in a three-team ladder match in September 2016?

10. To date only one ladder match has been held in New Japan Pro Wrestling. In 2016, Michael Elgin captured the IWGP Intercontinental title from which fellow North America star?

WRESTLING RINGS TO WEDDING RINGS

Identify the wrestling couples

The wrestling world is no stranger to romance, both for storyline purposes and in real life. Let's see if you can remember these famous pairings.

1. Daniel Bryan is married to which fellow WWE star?

2. Triple H had a long-term relationship with which wrestler, prior to his marriage to Stephanie McMahon?

3. Edge had various storyline romances, but in 2016 he married which former women's star?

4. The charismatic Marlena was a storyline valet and manager for which real-life husband?

5. WWE women's star AJ Lee had storyline romances with Daniel Bryan and John Cena, but which former world champion is she married to?

6. NXT wrestler Buddy Murphy is engaged to which main roster star?

7. What is the name of Cody Rhodes wife, a former ring announcer for the WWE and occasional in-ring competitor?

8. Inaugural WWE Divas champion Michelle McCool married which wrestling star in 2010?

9. Japanese women's legend Akira Hokuto married which competitor in 1995; they are regularly considered among the country's biggest celebrity couples?

10. Announcer Renee Young is married to which WWE star?

ENTER THE SHIELD

WWE's most popular faction?

Since 2010 no WWE faction has proved as popular with fans as The Shield. Let's test your knowledge of this supergroup.

1. What year did the Shield first debut as a faction?

2. When the Shield first started, they were "mercenaries" for which WWE icon?

3. Which object did Rollins use when confronting Ambrose and Reigns, to signal their break-up?

4. Which member of the Shield owns the record of most eliminations in a single Royal Rumble match?

5. When facing the Miz and four others in a TLC handicap match, who filled in for an ill Roman Reigns?

6. Which Shield member was the winner of the first NXT championship?

7. Up to Summerslam 2018, Dean Ambrose holds the title for the longest US championship reign under the WWE banner (351 days). Whose record did he beat?

8. As of mid-2018, which member of the trio is yet to win a "Money in the Bank"?

9. When Seth Rollins left the Shield, which fellow group did he join?

10. To which overseas show did the Shield arrive by helicopter?

WHO WROTE THIS?

Do you know your authors?

There are hundreds of excellent wrestling books out there, but can you match the title to the wrestling personality that they were either written by or are about?

1. Have a Nice Day

2. A Lion's Tale

3. Pure Dynamite: The Price You Pay for Wrestling Stardom

4. Hitman: My Real Life in the Cartoon World of Wrestling

5. The Last Outlaw

6. Walking a Golden Mile

7. Controversy Creates Cash

8. Crazy Like a Fox

9. The Hardcore Truth

10. Listen, You Pencil Neck Geeks

THE ROCK SAYS ...

Trading insults with the best

The Rock is known for his verbal beatdowns on just about every WWE superstar he came across. But which wrestler, interviewer or personality was on the receiving end of these lines?

1. "You run around here looking like a big, fat bowl of Fruity Pebbles"

2. "You Got the Spinnerooni, the Dipsy Doodle and the Sufferin' Succotash"

3. "_____, with his Mickey Mouse tattoos and his 33-pound head"

4. "Yeah I remember you as a kid backstage _____ playing with your My Little Pony and picking your nose and wiping it on your shirt"

5. "The heavens opened up and God Himself spoke to you and said this: 'Bob...' 'But my name's Billy.' 'IT DOESN'T MATTER WHAT YOUR NAME IS!'"

6. "On this night 25 years ago, from the testicles of Vince McMahon himself, came something so horrifying it sends chills up and down the bodies of men all over the world! Tonight marks the birth of _____"

7. "If you are The Game, then quite frankly, you need to go back to the drawing board because your game absolutely sucks!"

8. "Look at The Rock's competition. Look at him! It looks like a big monkey came down here, took a cr*p, and out came ____ "

9. "The Rock knows exactly who you are! There's a green shirt, H on your chest, green mask ... oh you're the Hamburglar!"

10. "I gotta get in my Pick-up truck, drink some Steve-Weiser, listen to some Backstreet Boys..."

CRUISERWEIGHT CHALLENGE

Let's hear it for the little guys

Smaller wrestlers have delivered some of the finest matches ever seen. Here are 10 questions celebrating their achievements.

1. Which high-flying masked cruiserweight twice captured the WWE world title?

2. Japanese star Keiichi Yamada has wrestled as which red and white clad aerial master for over 20 years?

3. Liger had a notable feud over the WCW Light Heavyweight title with which former American football star in the early 1990s?

4. Which British star captured the WWE Cruiserweight title in 2017?

5. Which WCW star was known as the "Man of 1000 Holds"?

6. Which weekly WWE show is devoted to the company's cruiserweights?

7. Who captured the WWE Cruiserweight title at WrestleMania 34 in 2018?

8. Under which name did current WWE star Finn Balor capture the IWGP Junior Heavyweight title in Japan on three occasions?

9. Which two English wrestlers traded the IWGP Junior Heavyweight title in 2017?

10. Which country's light heavyweight title was established in 1942 and has fallen under the ownership of several different promotions?

NEW JAPAN LEGENDS

Talking Japanese

Time to test your knowledge of New Japan Pro Wrestling.

1. Which legendary grappler founded New Japan in 1972?

2. In which city is New Japan's headquarters?

3. Who was the first American to win the IWGP heavyweight title?

4. In which year was the first Super J-Cup, a light heavyweight championship widely considered among the greatest events in wrestling history?

5. Who is the longest reigning IWGP champion, 720 days from June 19th, 2016?

6. What is the name of New Japan's annual January show, their equivalent of the WWE's WrestleMania?

7. In 1991, which team simultaneously held the IWGP tag belts and the WCW tag titles?

8. Which team is the only one to hold the IWGP, WWE, WCW, TNA and ECW tag titles?

9. Which Japanese star has captured the IWGP title seven times?

10. Which two stars competed for the IWGP title in January 2016 before departing the company for the WWE that month?

GENERAL TRIVIA 3

More random questions to answer

By now you know the score – see how many of these general wrestling knowledge questions you can answer!

1. In 1991, who was the first superstar to win a third WWE championship?

2. When Braun Strowman and Alexa Bliss teamed up in the Mixed Match Challenge, what was their nickname?

3. Who was the first ever Raw draft pick?

4. How many times did the British Bulldogs win the WWF tag team titles?

5. What was the name of Ted DiBiase's long-suffering valet?

6. What was the name of 1980's star Koko B Ware's parrot?

7. Which WWE tag team champions were originally known as the Miztourage?

8. Which member of the Usos is married to fellow wrestler Naomi?

9. Which WWE superstar has a very public love for her cats?

10. Which music star famously accompanied Wendi Richter to the ring during the mid-1980s?

THE NATURE BOY

Diamonds are forever ... and so is Ric Flair!

Ric Flair is considered to be one of the absolute greatest wrestling stars of all-time. How much can you recall about the Nature Boy's fabulous career?

1. In which year did Flair make his professional wrestling debut?

2. What catastrophic event almost ended Flair's career in 1975?

3. Who did Flair lose the NWA world title to in 1983, before soon regaining it?

4. Which other "Nature Boy" did Flair compete with in the late 1970s?

5. Which other wrestlers formed the original Four Horsemen with Flair in 1985, and who became their manager?

6. In 1989 Flair engaged in a legendary series of world title matches with which long-time rival?

7. At which event did Flair win his first WWF world title?

8. In 2003 Flair formed "Evolution" with which three WWE stars?

9. Flair's final match came at WrestleMania 24. Who defeated him?

10. He is the only star to be inducted into the WWE Hall of Fame twice. In which two years?

I AM PHENOMENAL

The quiz that AJ Styles built!

By the middle of 2018 AJ Styles was firmly established as one of the WWE's biggest stars; how much do you know about his career to date?

1. From which city and state does Styles hail?

2. With which legend did Styles team in WWE under the name 'Y2AJ'?

3. In which year did Styles become the first TNA X Division champion?

4. On how many occasions did Styles win the NWA world heavyweight championship?

5. Which popular wrestling publication named Styles "Wrestler of the Year" in each year from 2014 to 2016?

6. Who did Styles defeat in 2016 to capture his first WWE world title?

7. Who defeated Styles at the 2017 Royal Rumble to end that title reign?

8. In July 2017 Styles captured the US title twice – who did he defeat on both occasions?

9. Styles captured the WWE title for the second time in which British city – the only time the belt has changed hands outside of North America?

10. Styles captured the IWGP title during his New Japan run in 2014. Who was the last American to win that belt before him?

WHO ARE YOU?

Identify the wrestling stars from these descriptions

Here are 10 fun facts about wrestling stars, past and present. See if you can identify them from the description!

1. Which charismatic star was billed as the son of a plumber?

2. Which WWE star was once billed as the American Dragon?

3. Which star attempted to buy the WWF title in 1988?

4. Which larger than life star once reportedly drank over 150 beers in one day?

5. Which decorated star was the first Intercontinental champion?

6. Which star was known as Mr WrestleMania despite losing almost two thirds of the matches he competed in?

7. Which star held a wrestling and rock cruise in October 2018?

8. Which current WWE female star has a blind pig called Larry Steve?

9. Which strongman wrestler competed for the US weightlifting team at the 1992 and 1996 Olympics?

10. Which female star has released various country music records?

OH CANADA

From the Harts to Jericho, the best of Canada

Canada has a long and proud heritage in professional wrestling, arguably as strong as that of its other North American counterparts. Here are ten questions to test your knowledge of that country's impact on the wrestling landscape!

1. Which legendary Canadian figure ran Stampede wrestling for half a century?

2. What was the name of the infamous room at the Hart family house where many wrestlers were trained and "stretched"?

3. How many times has WrestleMania been held in Canada up to 2018?

4. Canadian star Chris Irvine is better known as who?

5. Bret Hart and brother-in-law Jim Neidhart formed which tag team?

6. Diana Hart was married to which British wrestling star?

7. Which member of the Hart family tragically fell to his death during a live pay per view event in May 1999?

8. Bret Hart's controversial loss to Shawn Michaels at Survivor Series 1997 is better known by what name?

9. Which Canadian women's wrestler was a huge star during the WWE's Attitude Era, thanks to her feud with Lita?

10. Which Canadian won the WWE Universal title in 2016?

SIMPLY THE BEST?

The WWF champions – in order!

The WWF title was first formally established in April 1963. Can you name the first 10 **different** individuals to hold the belt, and, for multiple winners, the year their **first** title reign began – the brief 1979 disputed reign of Antonio Inoki is not included!

1. ?

2. ?

3. ?

4. ?

5. ?

6. ?

7. ?

8. ?

9. ?

10. ?

IT'S A NEW DAY

Don't you dare be sour!

The New Day have made a huge impact during their short run in the WWE. But how well do you know them, both as a team and individually?

1. What musical instrument does Xavier Woods play?

2. What is the title of the New Day's breakfast cereal?

3. Which WrestleMania did the New Day host? WrestleMania

4. What is the name of Xavier's YouTube gaming channel?

5. Which member of the New Day is famous for his miraculous Royal Rumble saves?

6. Which member of the New Day begins their ring intro on the microphone?

7. How many Intercontinental Championships has Kofi Kingston won, up to Summerslam 2018?

8. What surname did Big E use during his NXT title reign?

9. Who did the New Day defeat to claim their first WWE tag team title?

10. When the New Day became the longest-reigning WWE tag team champions, whose record did they beat?

ALL JAPAN WOMEN

The golden age of women's wrestling

For a decade from the mid-1980s to the mid-1990s, the All Japan Women's promotion was arguably the hottest in the world, thanks to an incredible roster of stars and amazing supercards. Let's test your knowledge of that promotion.

1. The tag team of Chigusa Nagayo and Lioness Asuka were collectively known by what name?

2. In April 1993 two giant inter-promotional women's events were held under what name?

3. With which future tag partner did Manami Toyota have a brutal hair vs hair match in 1992?

4. Which monster star captured the WWWA world title in November 1992?

5. Which leading Japanese star captured the WWF women's title from Alundra Blayze in 1994?

6. Akira Hokuto married which male Japanese wrestling star?

7. Aja Kong and Bison Kimura formed which tag team?

8. Which two stars engaged in the 1995 *Wrestling Observer Newsletter* Match of the Year?

9. 1994's Big Egg Wrestling Universe event lasted approximately how long?

10. Tag team partners Takako Inoue and Kyoko Inoue had what family relationship?

HART TO HART

The greatest wrestling dynasty?

The Hart family is arguably the most influential dynasty in wrestling history, thanks to over 70 years of active competition and an extended family network. Here are 10 questions about this influential family.

1. In which Canadian city did the Hart family grow up?

2. What was the name of Stu Hart's successful Canadian promotion?

3. Who was the eldest of Stu's wrestling sons?

4. Which Hart brother was the youngest?

5. Diana Hart married which wrestling star?

6. Jim Neidhart and Bret Hart are cousins – true or false?

7. Which 1980s British wrestler was named an honorary member of the Hart family due to his close ties with the group?

8. How many times did Bret win the WWF world title?

9. At which 1993 event did Bret team up with brothers Owen, Bruce and Keith?

10. From which wrestler did Natalya capture the Smackdown women's title in August 2017?

ALL JAPAN STARS

The best of the 90s?

All Japan was arguably the country's dominant promotion through the 1990s thanks to a group of incredible stars. Let's see what you know about this company!

1. Which Japanese legend co-founded the company in 1972?

2. Which four stars led the promotion through the 1990s?

3. The main singles championship in All Japan was comprised of several titles bound together under which name?

4. Which legend was the inaugural Triple Crown champion in 1989?

5. Which former Freebird became the first American to hold the Triple Crown in 1990?

6. Which tobacco-chewing Texan won four Triple Crown titles in the 1990s?

7. How many days did Misawa hold the title during his five reigns?

8. Which face-painted star of New Japan won the Triple Crown on three occasions?

9. In which year did Kenta Kobashi finally realise his dream and win the Triple Crown?

10. In 2000, Misawa and most top stars left All Japan to form which company?

THE MCMAHONS

Family feuds and sibling rivalry

The McMahon family reign in WWF/WWE has been filled with great on-screen moments as well as storyline feuds between Vince, Linda and their children. How much do you recall of these famous incidents?

1. In which year did Vince McMahon Jr buy the WWF from his father?

2. In which year did Vince McMahon win the WWF world title from Triple H, before vacating it a week later?

3. In 1999 Shane McMahon captured the European title by defeating which member of Degeneration-X?

4. Which WWF Diva did Vince have an on-screen affair with to spite his family?

5. In 2001, Shane directly opposed his father by purchasing which company?

6. What is the title of Shane's long-established entrance theme?

7. In October 2005, which controversial WWE star used his finishing move on all four senior members of the McMahon family?

8. In which year did Shame announce his resignation from the company, leading to many years out of the spotlight?

9. In which year did Stephanie McMahon officially marry Triple H?

10. Which WWE legend memorably poked fun at Stephanie after her plastic surgery in the early 2000s?

GENERAL TRIVIA 4

A few WWE facts

Back to a general selection of questions. Let's see what you know!

1. In his Highlight Reel chat show, what was the name inscribed on Chris Jericho's TV?

2. How many times did Booker T win the WCW World Heavyweight title?

3. Which colourful WWE superstar walks to the ring with huge inflatable "buddies"?

4. Who was the first ever Smackdown draft pick?

5. What does AJ Styles' tattoo display?

6. In which year did Ric Flair join the WWF for the first time?

7. *Total Bellas* is a spin-off from which wrestling reality show?

8. In which country was Bruno Sammartino born?

9. Which former wrestling diva has been married to both Marc Mero and Brock Lesnar?

10. Mike Rotunda is the father of which two WWE stars?

THE QUIZ OF JERICHO

"You just made the list"

Chris Jericho is a bona fide legend, having competed all around the world in a glittering career. How many of the following questions about Jericho's early career can you answer?

1. Jericho was born in New York but grew up in which Canadian city?

2. Jericho's father Ted was a professional in which sport?

3. Where did Jericho get his wrestling surname from?

4. He adopted the nickname Lion Heart while wrestling in which country?

5. In 1995 Jericho joined which exciting US-based promotion?

6. In Jericho's famous 'man of 1,004 holds' promo, which move did he list repeatedly?

7. In which inventive way was Jericho's arrival in the WWF portrayed?

8. Jericho won his first WWF Intercontinental title against which star?

9. Which two stars did Jericho beat to become the first WWF Undisputed champion in 2001?

10. In 2008 Jericho captured a then-record eighth Intercontinental title against which high-flying star?

KEEPING IT RAW

The "crown jewel" of WWE TV

Since it began in 1993, Monday Night Raw has been a showcase for all the major stars in WWE history. Here are 10 questions about this long-running episodic show

1. In which year was Monday Night Raw first broadcast?

2. Who competed in the very first Raw match?

3. During the Raw years, which two personalities held the title of WWF President before the position was retired in 1995?

4. During Eric Bischoff's 2003 run as Raw General Manager, he was forced to share managerial duties with two different wrestlers – name them.

5. In which year was the first brand extension, which divided stars between Raw and Smackdown?

6. At Raw 1000, which outspoken star captured his first Intercontinental championship?

7. In June 2011, which champion famously sat on stage at the end of Raw and issued a "pipe bomb" against the company and its key figures?

8. In 1997, who became the first man to capture the WWF world title on Raw?

9. After his emotional WWF title win in January 1999, Mankind grabbed the microphone and borrowed a line from which famous fighting film?

10. Who succeeded Kurt Angle as acting GM of RAW in August 2018?

STANDING (VERY) TALL

The giants of wrestling

Few sights in the wrestling world can match the appearance of a true giant. How much can you recall about these (literally) enormous attractions?

1. What nationality was Andre the Giant?

2. Which mammoth Argentinian wrestler competed in WCW in the early 1990s in a hideous bodysuit?

3. Giant Silva was part of which group of unusual characters during the WWF's Attitude Era?

4. What was Andre the Giant's billed height during much of his WWF career?

5. In mid 1990s WCW, Ron Reis appeared as which legendary character?

6. What was the billed height of Japanese legend Giant Baba?

7. Seven-footer William Morrissey competed in NXT and the WWE from 2013-2017 under what ring name?

8. In which year was the Andre the Giant Memorial Battle Royal introduced at WrestleMania?

9. Which giant Indian wrestler made brief appearances in the WWE in 2017 and at the 2018 Greatest Royal Rumble?

10. What is the real name of veteran wrestler Big Show?

INTERCONTINENTAL GREATS

A small step to immortality

Ten questions about the WWE's long-standing IC title.

1. In 2005 who became the oldest IC champion at 56?

2. In 2001 who became the youngest champion, at 23?

3. Between 1999 and 2009 Chris Jericho held the title how many times?

4. What year was the title first established?

5. Who was the first champion?

6. Which champion held the title for 454 days from June 1987?

7. Who competed in the classic WrestleMania III title match, and who emerged with the belt?

8. Why did Ultimate Warrior vacate his title in April 1990?

9. Which two-time champion has held the title for the most combined days?

10. Up to October 2018, how many times has Dolph Ziggler won the title?

BY ANY OTHER NAME

Do you know your nicknames?

By and large, most wrestlers have one or more nicknames by which they are well known. Can you identify the wrestler from the names provided here?

1. The Lunatic Fringe

2. The Lone Wolf

3. The Big Dog

4. The Eighth Wonder of the World

5. The Ninth Wonder of the World

6. Big Red Machine

7. Viper

8. The Deadman

9. The Boss

10. The A-lister

IT'S BOSS TIME

Making a Banks Statement

One of the most popular recent additions to the women's roster, Sasha Banks is now a forerunner in the division. Here are 10 questions about the "Legit Boss".

1. Which NXT faction did Banks form with Charlotte, Becky Lynch and Bayley?

2. What is the name of her finishing move?

3. Who is Banks' supposed "best friend" and on/off rival in the women's division?

4. Up to October 2018, how many times has Banks won the Raw women's title?

5. In 2016, Sasha and Charlotte were the first women to enter which match?

6. In which city did Bayley win the NXT title from Banks in 2015's Match of the Year?

7. In their famous "Iron woman" match, what was the final score between Sasha and Bayley?

8. When Banks was called to the main roster in 2015, on which brand did she compete?

9. In late 2017, Banks competed in the first ever women's match in the Middle East, against whom?

10. Which legendary star is Banks' wrestling idol?

E C DUB! E C DUB!

Extreme entertainment

In the 1990s an upstart promotion challenged the big two US promotions by providing a style of wrestling never seen before on the major scene. Welcome to ECW.

1. Before it became "extreme", what did the initials ECW stand for?

2. In which city was the famed ECW Arena?

3. Which veteran star was the first ECW champion?

4. Which hardcore wrestler would often smoke and drink on his way to the ring?

5. The Sandman had a brutal feud, including a storyline where he pretended to be blind, with which wrestler?

6. Which ECW star often told lengthy stories to try and unnerve his opponents psychologically?

7. How many times did the Dudley Boyz capture the ECW tag titles?

8. Johnny Grunge and Rocco Rock formed which extreme tag team?

9. Which high-flying superstar left ECW and debuted in the WWF as Flash Funk?

10. In which year was ECW closed, before its later purchase and revival by the WWE?

WHO REIGNS SUPREME?

The Roman Empire

Roman Reigns is one of the most divisive stars in WWE. Pushed by the company, hated by many fans – test your knowledge of this major star!

1. What relation is Reigns to former WWF world champion Yokozuna?

2. What are the nationalities of Reigns' parents?

3. In which year did Reigns debut on the main WWE roster alongside his Shield partners?

4. Which was the first title Reigns won in the WWE?

5. At which event did Reigns win his first WWE world title and who took it from him the same night?

6. How did Reigns' second world title run end?

7. Why did reigns disappear from WWE in June 2016?

8. Which former world champion is reportedly Reigns' wrestling idol?

9. Who did Reigns face in the main event at WrestleMania 34, the match receiving a very poor crowd reaction?

10. At which event did Reigns finally capture the Universal Championship?

GENERAL TRIVIA 5

A little bit of everything

No further explanation necessary, have a go at this selection of random wrestling trivia!

1. Edge and Christian are successful tag team champions together, but both have also competed in a tag team with which WWE legend?

2. Who was the first man to capture the NXT championship twice?

3. After holding the IWGP junior heavyweight title for 14 months Prince Devitt (Finn Balor) lost the belt to which rising Japanese star?

4. What is Kevin Owens' native language?

5. Which British star held the Ring of Honor world title for 545 days between 2007 and 2009?

6. Which team dethroned the Hart Foundation for the WWF tag titles in 1987?

7. Which patriotic star controversially wrestled as an Iraqi sympathiser and held the WWF title briefly in 1991?

8. Which two words are tattooed on CM Punk's knuckles?

9. Tammy Sytch is better known as which wrestling diva?

10. As of October 2018, which wrestler has competed in the most WWE pay per view events?

UNIVERSAL CHAMPIONSHIP

Raw's flagship championship

Introduced as the premier title for Raw superstars, the Universal Championship has a short but notable history – let's test your knowledge of this recently added belt.

1. Which superstar beat Seth Rollins for the first ever Universal title?

2. Only two Universal champions weren't in NXT, name them.

3. In what kind of match did Kevin Owens win his first Universal title?

4. On which WWE brand is the Universal title mainly competed for?

5. Which member of The Shield has never competed for the Universal title?

6. In which year was the Universal Championship first established?

7. How many days did Brock Lesnar hold the title for?

8. At which event did Lesnar capture the title from Goldberg?

9. How old was the youngest champion, Owens, when he won the title?

10. How old was Goldberg when he became the oldest champion?

TAG TEAM TURMOIL 1

Name these famous teams!

Can you identify these current and former tag teams from their component wrestlers?

1. Arn Anderson and Tully Blanchard

2. Marty Jannetty and Shawn Michaels

3. Michael Hayes, Terry Gordy and Buddy Roberts

4. B Brian Blair and "Jumping" Jim Brunzell

5. Afa and Sika

6. Nick and Matt Jackson

7. Booker T and Stevie Ray

8. Tom Zenk and Rick Martel

9. Jesse James and Billy Gunn

10. Ax, Smash and Crush

TAG TEAM TURMOIL 2

Which tag teams are comprised of these wrestlers?

Identify these current and former tag teams from their component wrestlers?

1. Butch Reed and Ron Simmons
2. Ricky Morton and Robert Gibson
3. Kenny Omega and Kota Ibushi
4. Kane and the Undertaker
5. Scotty 2 Hotty and Grandmaster Sexay
6. Jerry Sags and Brian Knobbs
7. Steve Austin and Brian Pillman
8. Beautiful Bobby Eaton and Sweet Stan Lane
9. Kane and Daniel Bryan
10. Gene and Ole Anderson

MANAGERS TO THE STARS

Ringside rebels

Check out your knowledge of these famous men and women that have accompanied their wrestlers to the ring!

1. When Paul Heyman accompanies Brock Lesnar to the ring, he's not described as "manager" but by which title?

2. What nickname was given to iconic manager Jimmy Hart?

3. Which WWF manager led both Stan Stasiak and Superstar Billy Graham to world titles?

4. Which manager and commentator was named *Pro Wrestling Illustrated* Manager of the Year four times?

5. Paul Ellering was most famous as the manager of the Road Warriors. Which similar-sized team did he manage in NXT more recently?

6. Who was the long-term manager of the Four Horsemen?

7. Which manager famously threw in the towel, ending Bob Backlund's WWF world title reign in 1983?

8. Who was manager of ECW World Champion Shane Douglas from 1996-1999?

9. Which female manager of the Bodydonnas won the 1996 *Pro Wrestling Illustrated* Manager of the Year?

10. Who managed Demolition and often threw salt into opponent's eyes?

THE SLAMMY GOES TO ...

Celebrating the WWE's official "awards ceremony"

For many years the WWF/E held an annual awards ceremony, which recognized not only great performances in the ring but also afforded lots of comic potential for alternative prizes. Let's see what you know about the Slammy awards ...

1. In what year did the Slammy Awards originate?

2. Who was the first "best single performer"?

3. Who won a Slammy award in 2015, despite being injured?

4. Which icon ran around the ring with plastic awards shouting "two-time Slammys!"

5. Which wrestler was the 2008 "Diva of the year"?

6. Who won the 2012 "lol moment" when he chucked John Cena's stuff into the harbour?

7. Who won 2013 "catchphrase of the year" with "Yes! Yes! Yes!"

8. In 2015, Brock Lesnar won "twitter hashtag of the year". What was it?

9. Shawn Michaels has won the most Slammys. How many?

10. In 1987, the nominees for "manager of the year" were Bobby Heenan, Mr Fuji, Jimmy Hart and Slick, but who won?

THE QUIZ OF JERICHO 2

"Answer this, you stupid idiot!"

How much do you know about Jericho's more recent career, from 2009 to 2018?

1. Which movie star knocked Jericho out at WrestleMania 25 in 2009?

2. Chris Jericho and Edge won the WWE tag titles in 2009. After Edge was injured, who took his place as Jericho's partner?

3. After Jericho had won the WWE title in 2010, which unlikely opponent cashed in a Money in the Bank contract and defeated him for the belt? J

4. Jericho left WWE in 2010 to pursue music commitments with his band. What is its name?

5. In 2012 Jericho caused controversy by kicking the national flag of which country, leading to a suspension and public apology?

6. Jericho was a host of which WWE reality series in 2015?

7. Who was the first person added to the List of Jericho in 2016?

8. Which former "best friend" turned against Jericho during a televised Festival of friendship in early 2017?

9. Jericho captured the IWGP Intercontinental title in 2018 from which Japanese legend?

10. What is the name of his long-running podcast?

THE STREAK

The Undertaker's amazing WrestleMania journey

Few stories in the wrestling world have lasted as long or gained more importance than the famous unbeaten "streak" enjoyed by The Undertaker at WrestleMania. Here are 10 questions covering some of the major moments from that run.

1. The streak began when Undertaker defeated Jimmy Snuka at which event?

2. At WrestleMania 13, Taker not only extended his streak to 6-0 but also captured the WWF title from which fellow giant?

3. Who did Taker defeat at WrestleMania's 14 and 20, the first opponent he faced twice during his run?

4. In 2006, he defeated Mark Henry in which gimmick match to go 14-0?

5. Taker captured the world title from which star at WrestleMania 24 in 2008?

6. Which wrestler did Taker beat at both WrestleMania 25 and 26, the latter in a streak vs career match?

7. Who is the only wrestler to face Taker three times during his undefeated run?

8. In 2003, he defeated two men in a handicap match – name them!

9. Who was the final wrestler to be defeated during the streak, taking the record to 21-0?

10. Who finally defeated Taker to end the Streak in 2014?

WOULD YOU STOP!

The great commentators

Televised wrestling matches can often be elevated to greatness by the commentary. Here are 10 questions about the talented men and women who talk us through the events.

1. Which wrestling manager was a long-time co-host with Gorilla Monsoon?

2. Which WCW commentator caused many viewers to switch over to Monday Night Raw in 1999 when he gave away Mankind's world title victory?

3. Which commentator had a heart attack during a live broadcast of RAW?

4. Which commentator and wrestler became Governor of Minnesota in 1999?

5. Which legendary announcer was the main presenter at WrestleMania between 1997 and 2009?

6. Which commentator usually wore a crown during broadcasts?

7. Which WWE personality has been voted "worst commentator" five times by the Wrestling Observer Newsletter?

8. In 2018, who became the first full-time female commentator on RAW?

9. Who was the main TV commentator for Stampede wrestling for several decades?

10. Which charismatic and outspoken colour commentator also served as a manager for numerous teams including the Midnight Express?

TWITTER TALK

Do you know your social media?

Twitter has become a popular platform for wrestlers to not only engage with their fans but also to promote events, further their storylines and even feud. Which wrestling personalities use the following Twitter 'handles'?

1. @FightOwensFight

2. @TrueKofi

3. @JCLayfield

4. @YaOnlyLivvOnce

5. @OfficialHTM

6. @Fightbobby

7. @TherealRVD

8. @MmmGorgeous

9. @JRsBBQ

10. @RonKillings

WCW TRIPLE CROWN

Capturing the gold in World Championship Wrestling

Between January 1991 and March 2001, nine men completed the triple crown of
WCW titles – the world championship, the US heavyweight title and the tag team
championship. Can you name these nine individuals and, for a bonus, indicate the
four men in this list who also captured the WWF triple crown (world title,
intercontinental title, tag team championship).

1. ?

2. ?

3. ?

4. ?

5. ?

6. ?

7. ?

8. ?

9. ?

10. Who won both?

BEST OF BRITISH

From Big Daddy to 2018's TV revival

The UK has been a hotbed of professional wrestling for decades. World of Sport televised grappling for 30 years, and following its demise, the industry started to thrive again in the 2000s. Let's see how much you known about the British scene!

1. In which year was wrestling first shown on ITV's World of Sport?

2. Which promoter ruled the 1970s and introduced his brother as Big Daddy?

3. Who was Daddy's masked nemesis, billed from Japan?

4. Which promoter spearheaded All Star Wrestling, which became the longest running British promotion by 2013?

5. Which Irish star was a big name in Britain before making it big in WCW and then the WWE, where he works as an agent and producer?

6. Which English star, who enjoyed a run of success in TNA and Ring of Honor, and retired in September 2018, is widely regarded as the greatest British wrestler of the past 20 years?

7. Which popular Scottish grappler earned a spot in Insane Championship Wrestling thanks to a series of promotional videos on Facebook?

8. British wrestler Rockstar Spud returned to WWE under the name Drake Maverick in 2018 to manage which tag team?

9. Which Scottish wrestler returned to WWE in 2018 to partner Dolph Ziggler?

10. In 2018, British wrestling was back on TV via which show?

GENERAL TRIVIA 6

A bit of everything!

Test your overall wrestling knowledge with this selection of trivia.

1. In which stadium was WrestleMania III held before a reported crowd of over 93,000?

2. The Miz's wife Maryse hails from which country?

3. Which two Australian wrestlers make up the Iiconics tag team?

4. Which New Japan faction was created by Tetsuya Naito in 2015?

5. Which controversial promoter was fired by WCW in 1993?

6. Pete Gas and Rodney were portrayed as rich college boy henchmen of which McMahon family member?

7. Smoky Mountain wrestling was formed in 1991 by which loudmouth wrestling manager and promoter?

8. In Mexican wrestling, what do the initials CMLL stand for?

9. Miss Elizabeth was living with which former WCW star when she tragically died in 2003?

10. Who was the famous publisher of the *Pro Wrestling Illustrated* family of magazines?

BOYS (AND GIRLS) OF SUMMER

Testing your knowledge of Summerslam

Summerslam is arguably the WWE's premier show outside of WrestleMania. How well can you recall the major stories that have taken place there?

1. In which year was Summerslam first held?

2. How many different countries have hosted Summerslam?

3. Who has competed at the most Summerslam events?

4. Who has suffered the most defeats in Summerslam history?

5. Between 2009 and 2018, the event was held at which two venues?

6. In which year did Davey Boy Smith and Bret Hart compete for the Intercontinental championship?

7. Who did The Rock beat at Summerslam 2001 to capture the WCW world title?

8. Which two wrestlers fought in a brutal Hell in a Cell match at 2008's event?

9. Who captured the Intercontinental title at Summerslam 2018?

10. Between 2012 and 2018 who competed in six out of seven main event matches?

OVER THE TOP

Let's get ready to (Royal) Rumble

The "Road to WrestleMania" typically begins each year with the Royal Rumble. Here are ten questions designed to test your knowledge of this annual event!

1. In which year was the first Royal Rumble held?

2. Which wrestler has competed in the most Royal Rumble events?

3. How many wrestlers typically appear at each Rumble?

4. In which year did Shawn Michaels win the Rumble from position 1?

5. Which competitor won the Rumble in both 1997 and 1998?

6. Who has eliminated the most opponents in a single Rumble event?

7. Who has eliminated the most opponents across multiple events?

8. Who won the first women's Rumble in 2018?

9. The Rumble has never been held outside the US - true or false?

10. Who is the only female wrestler to compete in both men's and women's Rumble events?

MORE NICKNAMES!

Identify these wrestlers from their nicknames

Big Dog, Mr Monday Night, The Boss – all powerful nicknames for current WWE stars. Let's see if you can identify the ten wrestlers below from their nicknames.

1. World's Largest Athlete

2. The Peoples Champion

3. The Total Package

4. The Cerebral Assassin

5. The Billionaire Princess

6. The Baddest Woman on the Planet

7. The Man That Gravity Forgot

8. The Rainmaker

9. The Queen of Spades

10. The Cleaner

CENATION CHALLENGE

What do you know about the WWE's franchise player?

For 15 years John Cena's been the biggest name in the WWE. Let's see what you know about the man who divides fan opinion like no other!

1. What is John Cena's real name?

2. Which female star did Cena propose to in the ring at WrestleMania 33?

3. Who did Cena fight in his first ever WWE match?

4. Early in his career, what words did John Cena wear on his brass knuckles?

5. In what sort of vehicle-based match did Cena once defeat Kane?

6. Which foundation does Cena famously patronize to help kids achieve their dreams?

7. The Rock accused John Cena of looking like a bowl of which cereal, due to his colourful attire?

8. Cena was once blackmailed to temporarily join which evil faction?

9. What item of clothing does John Cena wear to symbolise his patriotism?

10. JBL and Cena had a long feud during which Cena vandalised which of JBL's vehicles?

FAMILY TIES

Name the famous fathers of these wrestling stars

There have been many family dynasties through the years in professional wrestling, some comprising a dozen or more members. Can you name the famous wrestler who is father to these recent stars?

1. Terry Funk

2. Harry Smith

3. Curtis Axel

4. Randy Orton

5. Natalya

6. Bray Wyatt

7. Jimmy and Jey Uso

8. Cody Rhodes

9. Lacey Von Erich

10. El Hijo del Santo

WHO SAID THAT

Which wrestlers use these catchphrases?

By most yardsticks, a wrestler's popularity can be down in no small measure to his or her ability on the microphone. Great catchphrases and promos are the hallmark of many standout competitors. But who is responsible for these?

1. And that's the bottom line ...

2. Who's next?

3. Yes! Yes! Yes!

4. Easy! Easy! Easy!

5. You can't see me!

6. I am the game, the king of kings, the cerebral assassin!

7. Whatcha gonna do, brother?

8. You just made the list!

9. Feel the glow!

10. You're Fired!

WHO SAID THAT 2

More famous catchphrases

Time to once again test your knowledge of famous catchphrases and sayings – which wrestler is responsible for the following?

1. Ladies and gentlemen, my name is …

2. Rest. In. Peace.

3. What a rush!

4. This is my yard now.

5. Get these hands!

6. Goodbye *kiss* Goodnight *bang*

7. Delete! Delete!

8. I am phenomenal

9. Bang! Bang!

10. For the benefit of those with flash photography

GENERAL TRIVIA 7

Exploring the world of wrestling

A final round of questions covering all areas of the sport!

1. In which city was 2018's WWE Super Showdown?

2. Name the five main members of the Kliq?

3. Which Japanese stars were named as *Pro Wrestling Illustrated's* number 1 male and female of 2017?

4. Which well-received 1999 wrestling documentary featured storylines involving Jake Roberts, Mick Foley and Terry Funk?

5. Which three wrestlers have played the main role in *The Marine* movies?

6. Which famed shoot wrestler held the world title on six occasions, including more than ten years combined as NWA champion?

7. What career did Trish Stratus excel in before joining the WWF?

8. In which year was the National Wrestling Alliance founded?

9. TNA star Lacey Von Erich is the daughter of which former world champion?

10. Which controversial basketball star joined the nWo for a brief spell in 1998?

ANSWERS

THE OPENING BELL

1. World Wrestling Entertainment, 2. "Stone Cold" Steve Austin, 3. McMahon, 4. WrestleMania, 5. Vitamins, 6. Bulgaria, 7. Giant Haystacks, 8. New Japan Pro Wrestling, 9. Battle royal / Royal Rumble, 10. Bulldogs

GENERAL TRIVIA 1

1. Snake - Damien, 2. MTV, 3. 50, 4. Kurt Angle, 5. The Rock / Dwayne Johnson, 6. 1999, 7. Antonio Inoki, 8. Kairi Sane, 9. Bobby Heenan, 10. Edge

"FROM PARTS UNKNOWN"

1. Andre the Giant, 2. Hulk Hogan, 3. Rusev, 4. Cactus Jack, 5. The Undertaker, 6. Charlotte Flair, 7. Zodiac, 8. Hardy Boyz, 9. Alexa Bliss, 10. Damien Demento

WRESTLEMANIA HIGHLIGHTS

1. Muhammad Ali, 2. America the Beautiful, 3. Brock Lesnar, 4. Edge and Christian / Hardy Boyz / Dudley Boyz, 5. Ultimate Warrior, 6. 23, 7. The New Day, 8. Hulk Hogan, Steve Austin, The Rock, 9. Bret Hart and Shawn Michaels, 10. Mike Tyson

BIG IN JAPAN

1. All Japan Pro Wrestling, 2. Giant, 3. Steve Austin, 4. Fergal Devitt / Prince Devitt, 5. Jushin Thunder Liger, 6. Mitsuhara Misawa, 7. Bullet Club, 8. The Great Muta, 9. The Golden Lovers, 10. Rick and Scott Steiner

WHO ARE YOU?

1. Undertaker, 2. Ultimate Warrior, 3. Ricky Steamboat, 4. Kane, 5. Charlotte Flair, 6. Roman Reigns, 7. Bayley, 8. Christian, 9. Dusty Rhodes, 10. (Big Van) Vader

BRITISH INVASION

1. Wigan, 2. Loch Ness, 3. Paige, 4. William Regal, 5. Chris Adams, 6. Lord Alfred Hayes, 7. Adrian Street, 8. Will Ospreay, 9. Jack Gallagher, 10. Tyler Bate

THE WOMEN'S REVOLUTION

1. Paige, 2. Australia, 3. Asuka, 4. Snoop Dogg, 5. Finn Balor, 6. False – it was Charlotte, 7. Sasha Banks, Alexa Bliss, 8. The Riot Squad, 9. The Empress of Tomorrow, 10. Sara Del Rey (Sara Amato)

NXT! NXT!

1. 2012, 2. TakeOver, 3. Jinder Mahal, 4. Becky Lynch, 5. DIY, 6. Brooklyn, New York, 7. Dusty Rhodes, 8. Adam Cole, 9. The Ascension, 10. SAnitY

GENERAL TRIVIA 2

1. His initials (Randal Keith Orton), 2. 4, 3. Honkey Tonk Man, 4. John Cena, 5. 2016, 6. Donald J Trump, 7. Andre the Giant, 8. Dean Ambrose, 9. 1989, 10. Chris Jericho

BITTER ENEMIES

1. The Monday Night Wars, 2. 3, 3. Bret and Owen Hart, 4. Big Van Vader, 5. Kevin Owens / Sami Zayn, 6. British Bulldogs, 7. Kenny Omega, 8. The Iron Sheik, 9. Tiger Mask, 10. Pepper

THE MONDAY NIGHT WARS

1. The Outsiders, 2. She dropped the WWF women's belt in a trash can, 3. Spray paint them with the nWo initials, 4. Disney Studios, 5. Vince Russo, 6. Goldberg, 7. Mankind defeating the Rock, 8. Kevin Nash and Hulk Hogan, 9. 84, 10. Lex Luger

YOU DESERVE IT ...

1. Bayley, 2. Kurt Angle, 3. "We want tables", 4. Stone Cold Steve Austin, 5. Ric and Charlotte Flair, 6. Brie Bella, Bryan's husband, 7. Chris Jericho, 8. Tommaso Ciampa and Johnny Gargano, 9. ECW ("E-C-DUB, E-C-DUB"), 10. Ole

HOGAN AND FLAIR

1. Iron Sheik, 2. you gotta beat the man, 3. Randy Savage, 4. Dusty Rhodes, 5. Kerry, 6. Andre the Giant, 7. Zeus, 8. Sting, 9. King Kong Bundy, Andre the Giant (twice), Randy Savage, 10. Sting, Great Muta, Lex Luger

THE HEARTBREAK KID

1. Razor Ramon, 2. Marty Jannetty, 3. Bret Hart, 4. Ric Flair, 5. His smile, 6. The Barber Shop, 7. WrestleMania 25 and 26, 8. Michael Shawn Hickenbottom, 9. Diesel (Kevin Nash), 10. 2011, Triple H

TABLES, LADDERS AND CHAIRS (OH MY)

1. WrestleMania X (10), 2. Edge and Christian, Hardy Boyz, Dudley Boyz, 3. Money in the Bank, 4. Rob Van Dam and Jeff Hardy, 5. Stampede, 6. Undertaker, 7. Becky Lynch and Alexa Bliss, 8. Chris Benoit and Jeff Jarrett, 9. Young Bucks, 10. Kenny Omega

WRESTLING RINGS TO WEDDING RINGS

1. Brie Bella, 2. Chyna, 3. Beth Phoenix, 4. Goldust / Dustin Rhodes, 5. CM Punk, 6. Alexa Bliss, 7. Brandi Rhodes, 8. Undertaker, 9. Kensuke Sasaki, 10. Dean Ambrose

ENTER THE SHIELD

1. 2012, 2. CM Punk, 3. A steel chair, 4. Roman Reigns, 5. Kurt Angle, 6. Seth Rollins, 7. MVP, 8. Roman Reigns, 9. The Authority, 10. Monday Night Raw in Manchester, England

WHO WROTE THIS?

1. Mick Foley, 2. Chris Jericho, 3. Dynamite Kid / Tom Billington, 4. Bret Hart, 5. Stan Hansen, 6. William Regal, 7. Eric Bischoff, 8. Brian Pillman, 9. Bob Holly, 10. Fred Blassie

THE ROCK SAYS ...

1. John Cena, 2. Booker T, 3. Undertaker, 4. Randy Orton, 5. Billy Gunn, 6. Stephanie McMahon, 7. Triple H, 8. Mankind, 9. The Hurricane, 10. Steve Austin

CRUISERWEIGHT CHALLENGE

1. Rey Mysterio Jr, 2. Jushin Thunder Liger, 3. Brian Pillman, 4. Neville, 5. Dean Malenko, 6. 205 Live, 7. Cedric Alexander, 8. Prince Devitt, 9. Will Ospreay and Marty Scurll, 10. Mexico

NEW JAPAN LEGENDS

1. Antonio Inoki, 2. Tokyo, 3. Big Van Vader, 4. 1994, 5. Kazuchika Okada, 6. Wrestle Kingdom, 7. Steiner Brothers, 8. Dudley Boyz (Team 3D), 9. Hiroshi Tanahashi, 10. AJ Styles and Shinsuke Nakamura

GENERAL TRIVIA 3

1. Hulk Hogan, 2. Team Little Big, 3. Undertaker, 4. 1, 5. Virgil, 6. Frankie, 7. The B team (Curtis Axel and Bo Dallas), 8. Jimmy Uso, 9. Natalya, 10. Cyndi Lauper

THE NATURE BOY

1. 1972, 2. An airplane crash in which he suffered a broken back, 3. Harley Race, 4. Buddy Rogers, 5. Arn Anderson, Ole Anderson, Tully Blanchard, with JJ Dillon managing, 6. Ricky Steamboat, 7. 1992 Royal Rumble, 8. Triple H, Batista, Randy Orton, 9. Shawn Michaels, 10. 2008 and 2012

I AM PHENOMENAL

1. Gainesville, Georgia, 2. Chris Jericho, 3. 2002, 4. 3, 5. Wrestling Observer newsletter, 6. Dean Ambrose, 7. John Cena, 8. Kevin Owens, 9. Manchester, 10. Brock Lesnar

WHO ARE YOU?

1. Dusty Rhodes, 2. Daniel Bryan, 3. Ted DiBiase, 4. Andre the Giant, 5. Pat Patterson, 6. Shawn Michaels, 7. Chris Jericho, 8. Alexa Bliss, 9. Mark Henry, 10. Mickie James

OH CANADA

1. Stu Hart, 2. The Dungeon, 3. 2, 4. Chris Jericho, 5. Hart Foundation, 6. Davey Boy Smith / British Bulldog, 7. Owen Hart, 8. The Montreal Screwjob, 9. Trish Stratus, 10. Kevin Owens

SIMPLY THE BEST?

1. Buddy Rogers (1963), 2. Bruno Sammartino (1963), 3. Ivan Koloff (1971), 4. Pedro Morales (1971), 5. Stan Stasiak (1973), 6. Superstar Billy Graham (1977), 7. Bob Backlund (1978), 8. The Iron Sheik (1983), 9. Hulk Hogan (1984), 10. Andre the Giant (1988)

IT'S A NEW DAY

1. The trombone, 2. Booty-Os, 3. WrestleMania 33, 4. UpUpDownDown, 5. Kofi Kingston, 6. Big E, 7. 4, 8. Langston, 9. Tyson Kidd and Cesaro, 10. Demolition

ALL JAPAN WOMEN

1. Crush Gals, 2. Dreamslam I and II, 3. Toshiyo Yamada, 4. Aja Kong, 5. Bull Nakano, 6. Kensuke Sasaki, 7. Jungle Jack, 8. Manami Toyota and Kyoko Inoue, 9. 10 hours, 10. None

HART TO HART

1. Calgary, 2. Stampede, 3. Smith Hart, 4. Owen Hart, 5. Davey Boy Smith, 6. False – they are brothers-in-law, as Neidhart married Bret's sister Ellie, 7. Dynamite Kid, 8. Five, 9. Survivor Series, 10. Naomi

ALL JAPAN STARS

1. Shohei 'Giant' Baba, 2. Mitsuhara Misawa, Toshiaki Kawada, Akira Taue, Kenta Kobashi, 3. Triple Crown, 4. Jumbo Tsuruta, 5. Terry Gordy, 6. Stan Hansen, 7. 1,799, 8. The Great Muta, 9. 1996, 10. Pro Wrestling Noah

THE MCMAHONS

1. 1982, 2. 1999, 3. X-Pac, 4. Trish Stratus, 5. WCW, 6. Here Comes the Money, 7. Stone Cold Steve Austin, 8. 2009, 9. 2003, 10. Chris Jericho

GENERAL TRIVIA 4

1. Jeritron 5000, 2. 5, 3. Bayley, 4. The Rock, 5. His children's birth dates, 6. 1991, 7. Total Divas, 8. Italy, 9. Sable, 10. Bray Wyatt and Bo Dallas

THE QUIZ OF JERICHO

1. Winnipeg, 2. Ice hockey, 3. An album called Walls of Jericho by rock band Helloween, 4. Mexico, 5. ECW, 6. Armbar, 7. By a Millennium countdown clock, 8. Chyna, 9. Steve Austin and The Rock, 10. Jeff Hardy

KEEPING IT RAW

1. 1993, 2. Yokozuna and Koko B Ware, 3. Jack Tunney and Gorilla Monsoon, 4. Stone Cold Steve Austin and Mick Foley, 5. 2002, 6. The Miz, 7. CM Punk, 8. Sycho Sid, 9. Rocky, 10. Baron Corbin

STANDING (VERY) TALL

1. French, 2. El Gigante, 3. The Oddities, 4. 7 feet 4 inches, 5. The Yeti, 6. 6 feet 10 inches, 7. Big Cass, 8. 2014, 9. The Great Khali, 10. Paul Wight

INTERCONTINENTAL GREATS

1. Ric Flair, 2. Jeff Hardy, 3. 9, 4. 1979, 5. Pat Patterson, 6. Honky Tonk Man, 7. Ricky Steamboat beat Randy Savage, 8. He won the WWF world title, 9. Pedro Morales, 10. 6

BY ANY OTHER NAME

1. Dean Ambrose, 2. Baron Corbin, 3. Roman Reigns, 4. Andre the Giant, 5. Chyna, 6. Kane, 7. Randy Orton, 8. The Undertaker, 9. Sasha Banks, 10. The Miz

IT'S BOSS TIME

1. Four Horsewomen, 2. Banks Statement, 3. Bayley, 4. 4, 5. Hell in a Cell, 6. Brooklyn, New York, 7. Bayley won 3-2, 8. Raw, 9. Alexa Bliss, 10. Eddie Guerrero

E C DUB! E C DUB!

1. Eastern Championship Wrestling, 2. Philadelphia, 3. Jimmy Snuka, 4. The Sandman, 5. Tommy Dreamer, 6. Raven, 7. 8, 8. Public Enemy, 9. 2 Cold Scorpio, 10. 2001

WHO REIGNS SUPREME?

1. Cousin, 2. Samoan and Italian, 3. 2012, 4. Tag team title with Seth Rollins, 5. Survivor Series 2015, Sheamus, 6. He lost the title when eliminated from the 2016 Royal Rumble, 7. He violated the Wellness Policy and was suspended for 30 days, 8. Bret Hart, 9. Brock Lesnar, 10. SummerSlam 2018

GENERAL TRIVIA 5

1. Chris Jericho, 2. Samoa Joe, 3. Kota Ibushi, 4. French, 5. Nigel McGuinness, 6. Strike Force, 7. Sgt Slaughter, 8. Drug Free, 9. Sunny, 10. Kane, with 173 appearances

UNIVERSAL CHAMPIONSHIP

1. Finn Balor, 2. Goldberg and Brock Lesnar, 3. Fatal Four Way, 4. Raw, 5. Dean Ambrose, 6. 2016, 7. 504, 8. WrestleMania 33, 9. 32, 10. 50

TAG TEAM TURMOIL 1

1. Brain Busters, 2. The Rockers, 3. The Fabulous Freebirds, 4. The Killer Bees, 5. The Wild Samoans, 6. The Young Bucks, 7. Harlem Heat, 8. Can-Am Connection, 9. New Age Outlaws, 10. Demolition

TAG TEAM TURMOIL 2

1. Doom, 2. Rock 'n' Roll Express, 3. The Golden Lovers, 4. Brothers of Destruction, 5. Too Cool, 6. Nasty Boys, 7. Hollywood Blonds, 8. Midnight Express, 9. Team Hell No, 10. The Minnesota Wrecking Crew

MANAGERS TO THE STARS

1. Advocate, 2. Mouth of the South, 3. The Grand Wizard, 4. Bobby Heenan, 5. Authors of Pain, 6. JJ Dillon, 7. Arnold Skaaland, 8. Francine, 9. Sunny, 10. Mr Fuji

THE SLAMMY GOES TO ...

1. 1986, 2. Junkyard Dog, 3. Seth Rollins, 4. Owen Hart, 5. Beth Phoenix, 6. The Rock, 7. Daniel Bryan, 8. #Suplexcity, 9. 11, 10. It wasn't given!

THE QUIZ OF JERICHO 2

1. Mickey Rourke, 2. Big Show, 3. Jack Swagger, 4. Fozzy, 5. Brazil, 6. Tough Enough, 7. Mick Foley, 8. Kevin Owens, 9. Tetsuya Naito, 10. Talk is Jericho

THE STREAK

1. WrestleMania VII in 1991, 2. Sycho Sid (Sid Vicious), 3. Kane, 4. Casket match, 5. Edge, 6. Shawn Michaels, 7. Triple H, 8. A-Train and Big Show, 9. CM Punk, 10. Brock Lesnar

WOULD YOU STOP!

1. Bobby Heenan, 2. Tony Schiavone, 3. Jerry Lawler, 4. Jesse Ventura, 5. Jim Ross, 6. Jerry Lawler, 7. Michael Cole, 8. Renee Young, 9. Ed Whalen, 10. Jim Cornette

TWITTER TALK

1. Kevin Owens, 2. Kofi Kingston, 3. JBL / Bradshaw, 4. Liv Morgan, 5. Honky Tonk Man, 6. Bobby Lashley, 7. Rob Van Dam, 8. Tyler Breeze, 9. Jim Ross, 10. R-Truth

WCW TRIPLE CROWN

1. Ric Flair, 2. Lex Luger, 3. Sting, 4. Diamond Dallas Page, 5. Goldberg, 6. Bret Hart, 7. Chris Benoit, 8. Scott Steiner, 9. Booker T, 10. Won both – Flair, Hart, Booker T, Benoit

BEST OF BRITISH

1. 1955, 2. Max Crabtree, 3. Kendo Nagasaki, 4. Brian Dixon, 5. Dave 'Fit' Finlay, 6. Doug Williams, 7. Grado, 8. Authors of Pain, 9. Drew McIntyre, 10.WOS

GENERAL TRIVIA 6

1. Pontiac Silverdome, 2. Canada, 3. Billie Kay and Peyton Royce, 4. Los Ingobernables de Japon, 5. Bill Watts, 6. Shane McMahon, 7. Jim Cornette, 8. Consejo Mundial de Lucha Libre, 9. Lex Luger, 10. Bill Apter

BOYS (AND GIRLS) OF SUMMER

1. 1988, 2. 3 - US, Canada, UK, 3. Undertaker - 16, 4. John Cena - 9, 5. Staples Center (Los Angeles) and Barclays Center (New York), 6. 1992, 7. Booker T, 8. Undertaker and Edge, 9. Seth Rollins, 10. Brock Lesnar

OVER THE TOP

1. 1988, 2. Kane - 19 Rumbles (plus three other matches), 3. 30, 4. 1995, 5. Stone Cold Steve Austin, 6. Roman Reigns (2014, 12 eliminations), 7. Kane - 44, 8. Asuka, 9. False, the first event was held in Hamilton, Ontario, Canada, 10. Beth Phoenix

MORE NICKNAMES!

1. Big Show, 2. The Rock, 3. Lex Luger, 4. Triple H, 5. Stephanie McMahon, 6. Ronda Rousey, 7. Adrian Neville, 8. Kazuchika Okada, 9. Shayna Baszler, 10. Kenny Omega

CENATION CHALLENGE

1. John Cena, 2. Nikki Bella, 3. Kurt Angle, 4. Word life, 5. Ambulance match, 6. Make-a-Wish, 7. Fruity Pebbles, 8. Nexus, 9. Army dog tags, 10. Limousine

FAMILY TIES

1. Dory Funk Sr., 2. Davey Boy Smith, 3. "Mr Perfect" Curt Hennig, 4. "Cowboy" Bob Orton, 5. Jim "Anvil" Neidhart, 6. Mike Rotunda (IRS), 7. Rikishi, 8. Dusty Rhodes, 9. Kerry Von Erich, 10. Santo

WHO SAID THAT

1. Steve Austin, 2. Goldberg, 3. Daniel Bryan, 4. Big Daddy, 5. John Cena, 6. Triple H, 7. Hulk Hogan, 8. Chris Jericho, 9. Naomi, 10. Mr McMahon

WHO SAID THAT 2

1. Paul Heyman, 2. The Undertaker, 3. Road Warriors / Legion of Doom, 4. Roman Reigns, 5. Braun Strowman, 6. Kenny Omega, 7. Matt Hardy, 8. AJ Styles, 9. Cactus Jack, 10. Edge and Christian

GENERAL TRIVIA 7

1. Melbourne, Australia, 2. Scott Hall, Kevin Nash, Triple H, Shawn Michaels, Sean Waltman (X-Pac), 3. Kazuchika Okada and Asuka, 4. Beyond the Mat, 5. John Cena, Ted DiBiase Jr and The Miz, 6. Lou Thesz, 7. Fitness model, 8. 1948, 9. Kerry Von Erich, 10. Dennis Rodman

ALSO AVAILABLE

Canvas Countdown: The World of Wrestling in 100 Lists is available now at Amazon. Both Kindle and paperback formats are available.

https://www.amazon.co.uk/Canvas-Countdown-world-wrestling-lists-ebook/dp/B079V7PNK

If you've enjoyed this, why not pop by www.PaulMeehanAuthor.com and leave feedback or sign up for some exclusive previews and updates on forthcoming books!

Thank you for reading!

Printed in Great Britain
by Amazon

32951554R00050